What The Bible Has To Say Abou

Introduction

Some people think the Bible has nothing to say about homosexuality and quite possibly think God is allowing it to happen because there are so many people who have been led astray by this movement.

Many voices, including President Barack Obama, talk shows and other civic leaders say that homosexuals have rights and should be allowed to do what they want. Even certain churches subscribe to this belief by allowing these individuals to have authority in their churches by leading Bible study, singing or leading the choir.

Whatever is going on in the world, and no matter how many people are doing it, you have to stand back and ask, "What does God have to say about this?"

I hear a lot of people say that God is a God of love and if you talk against homosexuals, you are not operating in love. These same people believe homosexuals should be allowed the same privileges as minorities or black people who were fighting for their rights in the 1960s and early 1970s during the civil rights movement.

Some may use the excuse that they were born this way and therefore they are not responsible for their behavior. I will answer and deal with all of these views and thoughts from the Bible's perspective. I will be both using the King James Version (KJV) as well as the New King James Version (NKJV) of the Bible.

It is my prayer Lord that everyone who reads this book will read with the mind of Christ (Phil. 2:5) with their eyes being opened to the move and will of God (Acts 9:1-18); and will break up the fallow ground so they may receive (Jer. 4:3; Hos. 10:12). May their eyes also be enlightened that they may see and know the will of God (Eph. 1:17-19).

Chapter 1

Creation

First of all, let's look at how God created man. In Genesis 1:26, God said let us make man in our image, after our likeness and let them have dominion over all living things. Now, to totally understand this you must know what God is. In John. 4:24, the Bible says that God is a Spirit.

A spirit cannot truly be seen by the human eye. So, what we are at the core is spirit. When God breathed into man the breath of life, that was God's Spirit going into man so that he would become a living soul according to the KJV. The NKJV says living being. But soul is a better rendering of that verse.

Soul in the Hebrew is *nephesh* (pronounced neh'-fesh). This means breathing creature i.e. animal or fig. sense (bodily or mental); any appetite, beast, body, breath, creature, lust, man, me, mind, mortally, one, own, person, pleasure, self.

Once again, this is where we get our thoughts, lusts, desires, and mind from. This is a very deep word. As you can see from the rendering of the word in Hebrew, even animals have a soul. Every living creature has a soul, and of course man has a soul.

But what separates man from the animals and every other creature is the spirit.

When the Spirit of God leaves man, he will die. This is seen in Luke 23:46, where Jesus is dying on the cross, gives His Spirit to God and breathes his last breath. The Greek word for spirit is *pneuma*. This means the human spirit, the spirit of the devil and the Holy Spirit. The KJV uses the word Holy Ghost to symbolize the Spirit because it is not seen by the human eye.

There are three types of spirits that you have to contend with. The human spirit, which allows us to communicate with God. Jesus said in Mark's gospel that He sighed deeply in His spirit, and said "why does this generation seek a sign?" That was Jesus the man, talking to the Father God about signs. In 1 Chronicles 9:4, the queen of Sheba went up to see King Solomon, who she had heard a lot about, to see if what she heard was true. After she saw, there was no more spirit in her. This means that she just could not believe it.

The final example of man's spirit is found in Romans 8:16 where it says, "The Spirit Himself (meaning the Holy Spirit) bears witness with our spirit (man's spirit) that we are children of God."

Then there's the spirit of the devil. This is evident in: Leviticus 20:27, where it says, "a man also or woman that hath a familiar spirit or (evil spirit) or that is a wizard, shall surely be put to death." Or Mark 1:26 where Jesus has to rebuke an unclean spirit, which is the spirit of the devil, who later came out of him. Finally, another evil spirit that Jesus had to rebuke and ordered never to enter him again: (Mk. 9:25).

There is also the Holy Spirit, which is the third part of the Godhead. (Gen. 1:2); The Holy Spirit is the Spirit of God who is responsible for all creation (Gen. 1:2). The Spirit landed on Jesus like a dove and helps us to do what we need to do (Mk. 1:10). This is evident in the scripture found in Galatians 5:16 where it says: "I say then, walk in the Spirit, and you shall not fulfill the lust of the flesh."

The devil will talk to you all the time if you let him. You have to learn how to tell that liar to shut up. I will also discuss this in this next paragraph.

Jesus was also a man otherwise He could not be tempted in all points and still be without sin (Heb. 4:15). This is illustrated in Matthew's gospel starting in chapter four where the Spirit of God was leading Jesus (the man) into the wilderness to be tempted of the devil (Matt. 4:1). His body was hungry (Mt. 4:2). The tempter or (devil) came to Jesus at His weakest moment (Matt. 4:3) and said, "If you be the Son of God, make these stones become bread."

The devil knew that Jesus had spiritual power. But would He use it for good or use God's power for just something to eat? He defeated the devil with the word. "Man shall not live by bread alone, but by every word that proceeds out of the mouth of God." (Matt. 4:4).

The devil also tempted the woman in the Garden of Eden with something to eat (Gen. 3:6). Did not the Lord say to the man not to eat of the tree of the knowledge of good and evil? We are to live by every word that proceeds out of the mouth of God.

Therefore, she should have obeyed God's word to her and not eaten it. Similarly, the devil came to Jesus with the same temptation and that is why He said what He said.

Then he took Jesus up to the pinnacle of the temple and told Him to throw Himself down because the angels will take charge of You and bear You up lest You dash Your foot against a stone (Matt. 4:5-6). This is how men in the pulpit twist the word of God. (I will discuss this in greater detail later).

The serpent, representing the man of God, misquoted that verse found in Psalm 91:11-12. How would the serpent know to use that scripture unless he was once up in heaven with God? All wisdom was taken from him when he fell.

But before the fall he was once a mighty angel, the most beautiful in the kingdom of heaven. He was called the anointed cherub that covers. Then he described this angel's attributes while he was still an angel in heaven. Ezekiel 28:11 says, "You were the seal of perfection; (meaning, everything that the Lord makes is perfect.) Full of wisdom perfect in beauty. You were in Eden, the garden of God." Eden means to be soft or pleasant, to live voluptuously; delight self. It also says pleasure; Eden, a place in Mesopotamia; delicate, delight.

The Bible refers to Mesopotamia because this is where Abraham sent his servant to find Isaac a wife. (Gen. 24:1-10). God obviously saw something in this place or He would not have told Abraham, the man of God, to send his servant there. Eden is a place that God was pleased with. It was soft for the people who lived there, (meaning they didn't have to work hard). It was a pleasant place where man was able to live voluptuously. It was also the place of Adam's home. The definition of voluptuous in Webster's dictionary is: pleasure, delight, agreeably, hope, expectation, to will, wish, full of delight or pleasure especially to the senses; ministering to, relating to, inclining to, or arising from sensuous or sensual gratification. It also relates to music, poetry, dancing and narratives of the far away South Seas. So, as you can see, this word is full of meaning.

7

Therefore, the serpent void of wisdom during this time, tried to get Jesus to once again use His powers for stupid things. The reason being is that the serpent is void of understanding.

Ezekiel 28:13 says "You were in Eden, the garden of God"; (Apparently, there was a Garden of Eden in heaven first, prior to the one on earth.) "Every precious stone was your covering, the sardius, topaz, and diamond. Beryl, onyx, and jasper, Sapphire, turquoise, and emerald with gold. The workmanship of your timbrels and pipes was prepared for you on the day you were created." This means that up in heaven, the anointed cherub that covers, made beautiful music in the day that he was created. God created this angel to lead praise and worship up in heaven. Verse 14 says, "you were the mighty cherub that covers; I established you; you were the holy mountain of God. You walked back and forth in the midst of fiery stones. You were perfect in your ways from the day you were created."

Then there is this very important line, **"Till iniquity was found in you**." After iniquity was found in him, he became the serpent found in Genesis 3, which is the beginning of his problems when he fell as found in Isaiah 14:12. "How you are fallen from heaven O' Lucifer, son of the morning! How you are cut down to the ground, you who weakened the nations!"

Ezekiel continues "For you have said in your heart I will ascend into heaven, I will exalt my throne above the stars of God; I will also sit on the mount of the congregation on the farthest sides of the north; I will ascend above the heights of the clouds, I will be like the Most High." That was Lucifer's problem—he wanted to be as great as God. That is why he said I will sit on the farthest sides of the north and finally I will be like the Most High.

When you go north, you are going up. He wanted to be as far up as he could get. It also says "I will exalt my throne above the stars of God" meaning, he wanted to be higher than God's throne. Isaiah 14:15 says; "Yet you shall be brought down to Sheol (which is Hebrew for grave); to the lowest depths of the Pit. (The pit is the deepest part of hell.)

God is not here to watch over you when you do something stupid on purpose. The word of God says and if you drink any deadly thing it will not harm you (Mk. 16:18). Of course, that is if you do it by accident without knowing. If you do it on purpose, then you are tempting God (Matt. 4:7).

Finally, the devil tempted Jesus with worshipping him by showing Him all the kingdoms of the world and their glory. What did Jesus say? "Away with you satan; for It is written worship the Lord your God and Him only shall you serve" (Matt. 4:10).

This is exactly how the devil tempted the woman in the Garden of Eden. First, she saw that the fruit was good for food, *the lust of the flesh*; that it was pleasant to the eyes; *the lust of the eyes*; and a tree desirable to make one wise; *the pride of life.*

I said earlier that I would tell you how to tell that liar to shut up. This is how to do it. You have to do it with the word of God. That is what Jesus had to do and that is exactly what you will have to do as well.

Our soul is what houses the human emotions. This is where we get our wants and desires from. Nephesh is the Hebrew term for soul. It literally means appetite, pleasure, lust, will, mental capacity which is the same as the intellect.

In Genesis 2:7, God says that he formed man out of the dust of the ground and breathed into his nostrils the breath of life, and man became a living soul.). The soul is the second level of man.

The last level of man is the body. It says in Genesis 2:7 that God formed man of the dust of the ground. In Matthew 26:41, Jesus said to "watch and pray lest you enter into temptation. The spirit (or man's spirit) is indeed willing, but the flesh or (body) is weak."

Man is a triune being. When I use the word *man* here I am saying mankind. This includes the woman as well.

You must command the soul to magnify the Lord because the soul is what the devil has access to. Another way of saying soul is the mind or intellect. In the gospels, Mary said: "my soul does magnify the Lord" (Luk. 1:46). Jesus said: "you must love God with all your soul" (Luk. 10:27). God is not going to do this for you; you must do it.

Then in Genesis 2:18, God says that "it is not good that man should be alone; so I will make a help meet for him."

When God said that He will make a help meet for man, this simply means that the woman will be able to *help* the man. The man is no longer alone because he has a woman to keep him company. When he has to perform his work, she will be there to help him with that too. Women have the ability to inspire and persuade men to do things.

Adam had to watch and keep the land (Gen. 2:15). During this time, there was still no helper for Adam so God caused a deep sleep to come upon Adam (Gen. 2:21). Then God took a rib out of man.

After Eve is created God performed the first marriage. When God says in Genesis 2:24:

"Therefore shall a man leave his father and his mother, and shall cleave unto his wife; and they shall be one flesh" this is the ultimate guideline that all marriages should follow according to God our creator.

In the most literal sense, God was both mother and father to the man and his wife. They left the platform of creation, if you will, and set out to keep and dress the land. (Gen. 2:15). The latter part of verse 25 says that they were both naked and were not ashamed.

Up until this time, the devil had not yet appeared and he had no authority over man. In other words, he had no control over man. Then in Genesis 2:9, God is telling you how He made every tree and food for the man and later on his woman to enjoy. Then at the latter part of the verse), God mentions the tree of the knowledge of good and evil.

Then God commands the man that of every tree of the garden you may freely eat; but He adds that the man not eat of the tree of the knowledge of good and evil because the day that you eat of it you will surely die.

When God says die, He does not mean die physically even though that will happen during the course of time but spiritual death would occur immediately.

Die is the Hebrew word *muwth*, which means to die, death, destroy or kill.

Remember that man is a triune being. He is spirit first and foremost. So, that is what died first. The spirit is what allows you to communicate with God.

King David, who probably prayed more than anyone because the book of Psalms are all about his prayers, said in Psalm 17: "hear a just cause O Lord, attend to my cry give ear to my prayer, which is not from deceitful lips." Prayer is how we communicate with God. Another way of saying prayer is talking to God. When David says hear a just cause O Lord, he means according to the <u>will</u> of God.

God's will before the fall of man was for man to dress and keep the land; (Gen. 2:15); not eat of the tree of the knowledge of good and evil; (Gen. 2:17); and be fruitful and multiply (Gen. 1:28).

After the fall of man, God's ultimate purpose was to seek and to save that which was lost. (Luk. 19:10).

The devil was finally introduced in the form of a serpent in Genesis 3:1, where it says that the serpent was more subtil than any beast of the field which the Lord God had made. The word *subtil* in the Hebrew means crafty, prudent usually in a bad sense. It comes from the word *aruwm* pronounced aw-room.

The serpent said to the woman in Genesis 3:1 "has God indeed said, You shall not eat of every tree of the garden?" And the woman said "we may eat the fruit of the trees of the garden; but of the fruit of the tree which is in the midst of the garden, God has said, You shall not eat it, nor shall you touch it, lest you die."

The first thing the serpent attempted to do is get the woman to doubt God. He asked her "has God indeed said?" That is the principle thing that the devil uses to get us to keep from receiving from God.

When Jesus was on the earth, He came in contact with a demon-possessed boy who was being thrown into the fire and the water in an attempt to kill him. (Mk. 9:17-22).

In the latter part of verse 22, the boy's father says, "if you can do anything have compassion on us and help us." Right there the man is showing _doubt_. Jesus knew it. This is why Jesus says what he said. Then Jesus responds with: **if you can believe?** That should be a question mark because Jesus is asking him a question. Then he follows that up with **"all things are possible to him who believes."**

If you have doubt, the devil will use that to trap you. The nation of Israel used doubt in believing that they could take Canaan. Moses sent a group of spies to spy out the land to see just how good the land was. (Numbers 13:1-2; 17-20).

Then it says that the men brought an _evil_ report back to Moses. (Gen. 13:32). The NKJV says "bad report." They both mean the same thing in the Hebrew. They kept on saying what they couldn't do (Num. 13:31). The report was evil because it was not according to faith. God would not send them out to do something that they could not do.

Then it says that "Caleb stilled the people before Moses, and said Let us go up at once, and possess it; for we are well able to overcome it." That is how God wants you to respond to that devil—with confidence and faith.

God never said they couldn't touch the fruit, just not to eat it. Therefore, the woman added to the word of God something that God never said. As soon as the woman added to the word of God, this gave the devil a _place_ into her life.

The Bible says in Ephesians 4:27 "nor give place to the devil." The word _place_ in the Greek is _topos_, which means place, opportunity, spot, license). When the woman added to what God said, she sinned without even knowing it. This gave the serpent **place or authority**.

Then the serpent was able to twist God's words and tell the woman she wouldn't surely die. If you don't know what you are talking about, the devil will be able to lie to you and get away with it. That is what the serpent attempted to do to the woman.

Furthermore, the serpent says "For God knows that in the day that you eat of it, your eyes will be opened, and you will be like God knowing good and evil." The KJV says it a little differently which is a better rendering of this verse. Instead of God, capital "G" it has gods small "g" knowing both good and evil.

With God being capitalized, this is absolutely out of the question. God is the only One capable of creating the heaven and the earth. (Gen. 1:1); creating man; (Gen. 1:27); and sending His Son to die for us (Jn. 3:16). The word "gods" on the other hand, symbolizes that there is more than one god in the world.

God said in the Ten Commandments that you shall have no other gods before me. (Ex. 20:3). Why would God say that if there was only one god in the world?

In the land of Egypt for example, they had a multitude of gods. This is illustrated in Exodus 12:1), where God executed judgment on Egypt by wiping out the first born of each family both man and beast and against all of the *gods* of Egypt.

Also in Psalm 96:4 it says: "For the Lord is great and greatly to be praised; He is to be feared above all _gods_." Then in verse 5 it says exactly what these gods are, "For all _gods_ of the peoples (or nations) are idols; But the Lord made the heavens."

The Bible also says in Revelation 22:18-19 that "if anyone adds or takes away from the prophecy of this book, (that being the Bible); that "God will add to him the plagues that are written in this book; and if anyone takes away from the words of the book of this prophecy, God shall take away his part from the Book of Life, from the holy city, and from the things which are written in this book."

It should be noted that the serpent did both. He subtracted the fact that Adam and Eve could freely eat from all of the trees of the garden, leaving out the tree of good and evil and added that they would be like gods knowing good and evil. God never said that—He said that they would surely die.

After the stage was set for them to believe a lie, it was now time for them to do exactly what God told them not to do in order for them to die.

In Genesis 3:6, the woman looked at the forbidden fruit, touched it and finally ate it. She then gave some of it to her husband and he ate.

After that, both of their eyes were opened and they knew they were naked. The devil has perverted everything the Lord made clean. As long as they were free from sin, they saw no problem being naked. But once sin entered the world, there was a big problem with being naked. No one had to tell them to cover up; they did it all by themselves.

The next thing that happens when you don't have God in your life is you get scared. They had no fear of God up to this point. Talking to God was like talking to your mother or father or a good friend. However, when they heard God coming through the garden, they hid themselves. In other words, they got scared.

God gave man and woman a test to see if they would tell Him the truth (Gen. 3: 9-13). These are just a series of questions that God asked. God knows all things and knew they were hiding and why. This is illustrated in Psalm 139, where it says no matter where I am your Spirit is there. You know my sitting down and my rising up. I implore you to read the whole chapter.

After God finds out what they did, He passes judgment on the serpent first and ends with the man (Gen. 3:14-19). It should be noted that up until this time, the woman was called *woman.* But after the fall, it says that "Adam called his wife Eve because she was the mother of all living" (Gen. 3:20). Eve in the Hebrew is *zirmah* meaning life giver or first woman. The word *woman* is Ishshah pronounced ish-shaw, which means wife, woman, each, every, female. This word is often unexpressed in English.

The Hebrew meaning of woman carries no definition of living. For something to be alive it has the ability to die as well. So, if Eve stayed according to the Hebrew rendering of that word, we would all have been Adam. This includes the woman as well.

The word *man* is pronounced <u>Adam</u> which means human being, species, an individual. Adam's name never changed even through the fall of man.

Chapter 2

Sodom and Gomorrah

In Genesis 12:1, God told Abram to get out of his country, from his family and from his father's house to a land that God would show him. In 12:4, it says that Abram left and Lot went with him. Lot was Abram's nephew (Gen. 12:5).

Then, there was a famine in the land and Abram and Lot went into Egypt (Gen. 12:10). Abram had a beautiful wife who he said was his sister when approached by Pharaoh. When the princes of Egypt saw Abram's wife, they saw that she was beautiful and took her into Pharaoh's house.

Then, Pharaoh treated Abram very well because of his wife and gave Abram sheep, oxen, male donkeys, male and female servants, female donkeys and camels In Genesis 12:15, God sent plagues to Pharaoh and his house because of Sarai his wife. Pharaoh wanted to know why Abram deceived him like that and sent him out of the land.

When Abram came out of Egypt he was rich in livestock, silver and gold (Gen. 13:2). Abram and Lot's men were fighting because the land was not enough to support them both. (Gen. 13:6 and 7).

In Genesis 13:9, they separated. Lot chose the plain of Jordan while Abram dwelt in Canaan. Lot eventually pitched his tent all the way to Sodom. The Bible notes that the men of Sodom were exceedingly wicked and sinful against the Lord. We will find out a little bit later why.

In Genesis 18:1, the Lord appeared to Abraham by the terebinth trees of Mamre as he was sitting in the tent door in the heat of the day. God will come to you when you least expect it.

Abram's name was changed to Abraham. First of all, Abraham, showed great faith. Abram in the Hebrew is Abram and it means high father while Abraham means father of a multitude. Up to this time Abraham and Sarah had no children. But God promised a son before it even happened. God told him to call his name Isaac (Gen. 17:19).

Genesis 18:2 says, "So Abraham lifted his eyes and looked and behold three men were standing by him; and when he saw them and went over to meet them, he bowed himself to the ground. Then he asked them if favor had been found in their sight do not pass by your servant."

Abraham knew that these were some important people so he offered them water to wash their feet and also something to eat before they went on their way and they told him to do as he had said.

In verse 17, God was about to tell Abraham what was going to happen to Sodom and Gomorrah. Genesis 18:20 says, "because the outcry of Sodom and Gomorrah is so great and because their sin is so grave, I will go down to see if the outcry is all of what I have heard it to be and if it is I will know, the Lord says."

Now Abraham being such a righteous man and not wanting the innocent to die with the wicked, asks the Lord several times if He would still destroy the city if there were a certain amount of innocent there.

Abraham let's God know that it was not like the Lord to kill or destroy the righteous with the wicked.

In Hebrew, *righteous* is *tsaddiyq* pronounced tsad-deek, which means just, lawful, righteous man.

That is what Abraham was—lawful, a man who kept the law; just; doing what is right and consequently could be seen as righteous.

In Hebrew the word *wicked* is raw-shaw which means morally wrong, bad person condemned, guilty, (man) who did wrong. These men of Sodom and Gomorrah were morally wrong, were condemned and guilty of sin by the Lord.

In Genesis18:24, there was a conversation going back and forth between God and Abraham. Abraham asked if there were 50 righteous people in the city, would He still destroy it and God told him no. God was showing love for mankind by not destroying the righteous with the wicked.

Then Abraham asked again if there are five less than 50 would He still destroy the city. God once again responded with no. This went on until verse 32 where Abraham asked one last time if there were just 10 people in the city would he destroy the place. God once again said no. Then the Lord went his way as soon as He finished speaking with Abraham and Abraham went back to his place (Gen. 18:33).

In the introduction, I raised the question: will God change his mind because everyone is led astray by the homosexuality movement? The answer is no. Sodom and Gomorrah decided to be gay or homosexual and God could not even find 10 righteous men in the whole city. The righteous were those who wanted to follow God instead of following satan or their flesh.

Abraham knew that God was too righteous to destroy the righteous with the wicked for David writes: "Who keeps our soul among the living and does not allow our foot to be moved" (Ps. 66:9). This means that God will not allow your soul to die, or those who are standing for God to be defeated.

In Genesis 19, two angels came to Sodom in the evening where Lot was sitting at the gate of Sodom.

Lot asked them to come in his house so they could wash themselves and leave the following day. They said no, they would spend the night in the open square. Lot strongly insisted that they come into the house; so they did and Lot baked them unleavened bread and they ate.

Then it says before the men laid down, the men of Sodom, both old and young, all people from every quarter, surrounded the house. That sounds like a lot of people to me. They called out to Lot and said to him where are the men that came to you tonight? Send them out that we may know them carnally. This means that they wanted to have sex with them. Once again, this is men with men!

Lot went out to them and closed the door behind him and told them not to do this wicked thing. Why he offered to give his daughters to these men outside is beyond me. But, he continued to tell them not to do this wicked thing since this is the reason why they came underneath his roof.

Then, the men tell him to stand back and are about to break down the door. The angels reached out their hands and pulled Lot into the house and shut the door. They then struck the men outside with blindness so they could not find the door.

When God strikes you with blindness, that is a form of judgment and He means for you to stop immediately what you are doing. The Apostle Paul also struck a man with blindness because he was trying to prevent someone from receiving the Lord (Acts 13:8-12).

Even Apostle Paul or (Saul) which is what his name was then, was struck with blindness because he was trying to destroy the church on the road to Damascus; (Acts 9:8)

In verse 12, which is the key verse, the men asked Lot if he had any family members there so he could take them out of this place. The angels said they were going to destroy the place because "the outcry against them has grown great before the face of the Lord, and the Lord has sent us to destroy it." God will give you space to repent, but after you do it so long and then try to force others to do it; God has no other alternative but to take you completely out of the picture.

Then when God sees that you are a righteous man and that he wants to save your life, he will send you help. In 19:16, the angels saw that Lot was still lingering so the men took his hand, the hand of his family and brought them outside the city.

This is a good time to say that you must pray over your family. Abraham's life was so full of God and prayer that God intervened on Lot's behalf, even though he was taking too long to move.

If that wasn't enough, Lot told them that he could not escape where the angels wanted him to go, which was up to the mountains. Apparently, Lot was smarter than God is because he was saying something different than what God said. But in this same chapter God told them not to look behind them, and that is exactly what God meant. So, Lot asked them to let him go to this small town, which he renamed Zoar . When Lot entered Zoar, God rained fire and brimstone on Sodom and Gomorrah.

Lot's wife still longed for Sodom and Gomorrah and ended up looking back; which the angels told her not to do. When she did she turned into a pillar of salt and died (Gen. 19:26). (Gen. 19:26). This whole city only wanted to be with other men. God saw that as wicked and judged them for it.

This is only my assumption, but maybe Lot's wife secretly wanted to be with other women, which is why she looked back. God knew that and killed her for it.

It should also be noted that this was all before the law. Now you may be asking yourself how could God judge them for something that hadn't been written yet? They just didn't know any better. But God said in Romans 1:20 that they are without excuse. God's very creation, the sun, moon, stars, firmament, our bodies, all speak of a Creator. In view of all that, God says you don't have an excuse.

In verse 24, God gave them up to uncleanness through the lust of their own hearts, to dishonor their own bodies between themselves.

The body was meant to glorify God, not have sex with another man or a woman with another woman. First Corinthians 6:20 says glorify God in your body and in your spirit which are God's. Jeremiah 17:9, says: the heart is deceitful above all things and desperately wicked; who can know it? You must watch your heart. The heart is like the body— whatever it can imagine, it will do regardless of whether it glorifies God or not.

Romans 1:26-27 says, "For this cause God gave them up unto vile affections; for even their women did change the natural use into that which is against nature; and likewise also the men, leaving the natural use of the woman, burned in their lust one toward another; men with men working that which is unseemly, and receiving in themselves that recompense of their error which was meet."

In other words, it was never meant for a man to be with another man or for a woman to be with another woman. Remember in chapter 1 I said that the ideal method for marriage is found in Genesis 2:24. If marriage does not follow this standard, then disease will set in. This is what is meant by recompense of their error which was *meet*. The NKJV says *due*.

There are many diseases that can happen as a result of a man being with another man or a woman being with another woman. These are commonly referred to as STDs or sexually transmitted diseases.

The first of these diseases is gonorrhea. This is a contagious disease that causes inflammation of the central mucous membrane caused by the gonococcus. This causes the vagina in women to be massively swollen and red, and the lower abdomen may be tense and very tender. In men, they have a very hard time urinating without experiencing a lot of pain.

The next disease is syphilis. This causes small painless red pustule on the skin or mucous membrane between 10 and 90 days after exposure.

Herpes genitalis is an infection caused by the type 2 herpes simplex virus, usually transmitted by sexual contact. It causes painful vesicular eruptions on the skin and mucous membranes of the genitalia of males and females.

Next is AIDS or acquired immune deficiency syndrome. This is when the whole body begins to shut down because the body is not producing enough antibodies, and as a consequence, cannot defend itself against anything. AIDS by far is the deadliest of the three diseases and most common among the homosexual population.

Judges 19:15-25 tells the story of a man and his servant on a long journey. They came to this town in Gibeah, which is where the tribe of Benjamin lived. These men are a little bit different because they appeared to be bi-sexual. This means that they liked men and women. Verses 20-22 say, "And the old man said, "Peace be with you! However, let all your needs be my responsibility; only do not spend the night in the open square." So he brought him into his house, and gave fodder to the donkeys. And they washed their feet, and ate and drank. As they were enjoying themselves, suddenly certain men of the city, perverted men, surrounded the house and beat on the door."

The Bible says they were perverted. Perverse in Webster's dictionary is defined as turning away from what is right or good. So, these were not good people. The KJV uses the word *belial* which means a title for a worthless man. In other words, they were wicked.

They spoke to the master of the house, the old man, saying "Bring out the man who came to your house, that we may know them carnally." Once again they wanted to have sex with him.

Judges 19:23-25: "But the man, the master of the house, went out to them and said to them, "No, my brethren! I beg you, do not act so wickedly! Seeing this man has come into my house, do not commit this outrage. Look, here is my virgin daughter and the man's concubine; let me bring them out now. Humble them and do with them as you please; but to this man do not do such a vile thing! But the men would not heed him. So, the man took his concubine and brought her out to them. And they knew her and abused her all night until morning; and when the day began to break, they let her go."

If you read on, the men of that town killed that woman and his concubine. Then, this man took a knife and cut up his concubine and cut her up into 12 pieces and sent her to the 12 tribes of Israel.

When the nation of Israel found out what happened they were very upset and wanted something to be done about it. So, the tribes of Israel fought the tribe of Benjamin (Jud. 20:14). Then they inquired of God who should fight against Benjamin first (Jud. 20:18). There was fighting going back and forth but finally in Judges 20:46 it says, "So all who fell of Benjamin that day were twenty-five thousand men who drew the sword, all these were men of valor."

If that wasn't enough, some of the tribe of Benjamin had run away so they were defeated as well. (Jud.

20:48). As you can see, a whole tribe of Israel was wiped off the face of the earth because they wanted to have illicit sex with other men and then committed murder by killing a concubine.

Chapter 3

Marriage

God has a lot to say about marriage and the role of the husband and wife. First of all, it was part of God's plan for a man to find a wife (Prov. 18:22). God also had a plan for how men should interact with women. Leviticus 18:22 says, "You shall not lie with a male as with a woman. It is an abomination." Also, there are a series of things you should not lie with all found in Leviticus 18. If you get a chance, read it over.

In Deuteronomy 22:5 it says, "A woman shall not wear anything that pertains to a man, nor shall a man put on a woman's garment, for all who do so are an abomination to the Lord your God." This pertains to transvestites who cross over and try to look and dress like a woman, which is strictly forbidden.

There are also transgender people who try to say God made a mistake by making me a woman when I actually should have been born a man; or a woman who says God once again made a mistake making me a woman, when I actually should have been born a man. Furthermore, it is also an abomination.

The Hebrew word for abomination is *tow'ebah* pronounced to-aybaw or toebah pronounced to-ay-baw meaning something disgusting morally i.e. (as noun) an abhorrence; especially or worshipping of an idol. Abominable custom, thing - abomination.

The Bible says in Hebrews 13:4, "Marriage is honorable among all, and the bed undefiled; but fornicators and adulterers God will judge." The KJV says whoremongers, but fornicators is a better word. Fornication fully demonstrates all of the things that cause this to happen. However, they pretty much mean the same thing. Also, it says that homosexuals will not inherit the kingdom of God (I Cor. 6:9-10).

Adultery is one of the things that can defile the marriage bed. This is when a man or woman, decides that he or she wants to have sex with someone while he or she is already married to someone else. This is found in Exodus 20:14.
It was also punishable by death according to the law (Jn. 8:1-5).

A man who leaves a wife through divorce commits adultery (Matt. 5:31-32). Even lust over another woman while being married equals adultery: (Matt. 5:27-28).

The word *fornicate* in the Greek is *porneia* pronounced por-ni-ah; which means harlotry including adultery and incest as well as idolatry. Porneuo means to act the harlot, indulge in unlawful lust of either sex; practice idolatry; commit fornication. It also means to sell, prostitute, fornicator or whoremonger.

There are a total of four different words in the Greek that make up fornicate. These are all of the definitions for those words. This is also where we get the word porno or pornographic from.

The Apostle Paul has some things to say about fornication too. In 1 Corinthians 6:18, where it says, "Flee fornication. Every sin that a man doeth is without the body; but he that committeth fornication sinneth against his own body." This means that every sin that a man does is usually against someone else.

For example, if you kill someone, lie or steal, that affects another person's body. It does not directly affect your body, although if left unchecked and not repented of, it will ultimately destroy you.

However, when you commit fornication with someone, it affects your body immediately. It is like the diseases that I discussed earlier. You open yourself up to so many different things.

In 1 Corinthians 7:1-4 Paul states that "it is good for a man not to touch a woman. Nevertheless, because of sexual immorality, let each man have his own wife, and let each woman have her own husband. Let the husband render to his wife the affection due her, and likewise also the wife to her husband. The wife does not have authority over her own body, but the husband does. And likewise the husband does not have authority over his own body but the wife does."

This simply means that the body is not completely controlled by you but you must sometimes do what the wife or husband wants you to do. If the wife wants to make love and you don't; you really don't have the right to say that I don't want to make love to you now.

If the man wants you to do the dishes, you don't really have the right to tell him that I will not do that. You are in this together and you have to work things out together.

Therefore, you can see clearly from these scriptures that the Bible never said that the man should have his own man and the woman should have her own woman. That would be against God's law and an abomination, which was discussed earlier.

Verses 5-7 continue: "Do not deprive one another except with consent for a time, that you may give yourselves to fasting and prayer; and come together again so that satan does not tempt you because of your lack of self-control. But I say that as a concession, not as a commandment. For I wish that all men were even as I myself. But each one has his own gift from God, one in this manner and another in that."

Do you really think that Paul could have written two-thirds of the New Testament and do all of the things that he did and all of the journeys that he made if he were married? This is one of the very reasons why he probably said this.

Finally, verses 8-9, "But I say to the unmarried and to the widows; it is good for them if they remain even as I am; but if they cannot exercise self-control, let them marry. For it is better to marry than to burn with passion. The KJV says just burn. "Burn with passion was added later."

This is the order of God concerning marriage.

In (Ephesians 5:22-23, God says, "Wives, submit to your own husbands, as to the Lord. For the husband is head of the wife, as also Christ is head of the church; and He is the savior of the body."

When the Bible uses the word *body* here it means the body of Christ. We are all here to do a work for

God. Just like if your body gets hurt somehow, your whole body feels it and attempts to come to the aid. Similarly, we are to come to the aid of each other, if we see a member of the Body of Christ hurting. If they need prayer, we should pray for them; if they need money and it is in our ability to help, we should help them with that too (I Cor. 12:12-27).

Verses 24-27 say, "Therefore, just as the church is subject to Christ, so let the wives be to their own husbands in everything. Husbands, love your wives, just as Christ also loved the church and gave Himself for her. That He might sanctify and cleanse her with the washing of water by the word. That He might present her to Himself a glorious church, not having spot or wrinkle or any such thing, but that she should be holy and without blemish."

This means that the husband being the high priest in the family should tell the woman when she is doing wrong so that she can serve the Lord faithfully. The high priest was the only one allowed to go into the Holy of Holies, and that being once a year, to pray for the sins of the people.

In Hebrews 9:11-12, Christ did this for us. But now we are able to do that very same thing because it says in Hebrews 4:16, "Let us therefore come boldly to the throne of grace, that we may obtain mercy and find grace to help in time of need." That throne of grace the Bible is talking about is the most holy place which only the high priest was able to go to in the Old Testament.

But after Jesus had died, that place where the most holy place was located was torn, which meant that we all have access to that place now (Mk. 15:38).

If the wife has a question about the Bible, the husband should be prepared to tell the wife what it means.

Ephesians 5:28-32 continues, "So husbands ought to love their own wives as their own bodies; he who loves his wife loves himself." (That is because they are no longer two people but one illustrated in Genesis 2:24), which is what I discussed earlier.)

"For no one ever hated his own flesh, but nourishes and cherishes it, just as the Lord does the church. For we are members of his body, of His flesh and of His bones. For this reason, a man shall leave his father and mother and be joined to his wife, and the two shall become one flesh. This is a great mystery, but I speak concerning Christ and the Church." That is because when Jesus was praying by Himself to the Father, he said in John 17:20-23: "I do not pray for these alone, but also for those who will believe in Me through their word that they all may be one as You, Father are in Me; and I in You; that they also may be one in Us, that the world may believe that

You sent Me. And the glory which You gave Me I have given them, that they may be one just as We are one. I in them, and You in Me, that they may be made perfect in one, and that the world may know that You have sent Me, and have loved them as You have loved Me."

Finally, going back to Ephesians 5:33, "Nevertheless let each one of you in particular so love his own wife as himself, and let the wife see that she respects her husband."

Therefore, if you do what has been outlined in this chapter, you will have a very successful, long and loving marriage.

Chapter 4

It Does Not Matter What People Say

God is not impressed with who you are, what you represent or how many people you are able to influence. If you are saying something that is against God's law, you shall be judged.

In the days of King Hezekiah, there was another king by the name of Sennacherib, who was the king of Assyria who had a lot of things to say against the God of Judah. He sent important people to speak to King Hezekiah.

In 2 Kings 18:17-19, it says "Then the king of Assyria sent the Tartan (a title probably a Commander and Chief); the Rabsaris (a title probably Chief Officer); and the Rabshakeh (a title probably chief of staff or governor) from Lachish, with a great army against Jerusalem, to King Hezekiah. And they went up and came to Jerusalem. When they had come up, they went and stood by the aqueduct from the upper pool, which was on the highway to the Fuller's Field. And when they had called to the king, Eliakim the son of Hilkiah, who was over the household, Shebna the scribe, and Joah the son of Asaph, the recorder, came out to them. Then the Rebshakeh said to them, Say now to Hezekiah, thus says the great king, the king of Assyria, what confidence is this in which you trust?"

This entire king's cabinet was in agreement with what this king had to say. President Obama, similarly, when he said that whether you be gay, straight, lesbian etc., you can make it here; is refusing to adhere to what God has to say about these people when He said that homosexuality is an abomination (Lev. 18:22 and that it is wicked (Gen. 19:6,7).

President Barack Obama said these things usually when he was making a public address to the nation. This is like when king Sennacherib sent all his advisors to the aqueduct from the upper pool, which was on the highway to the Fuller's Field. He also said it to King Hezekiah's staff as well (II Ki. 18:18). This was a public forum in which similarly, the Senate and House of Representatives meet to discuss important matters. In this case, gays and lesbians and anyone else living that type of lifestyle.

When the president said that, without him even knowing it, he was in effect saying: what confidence is this in which you trust? Meaning, he was questioning the God of this universe saying that this is wrong for God to feel this way towards gays, lesbians etc. However, the president is willing to consider this behavior alright. Also, the president is representing everyone in the United States, which is the army that was present in this day. (II Ki. 18:17).

The first thing out of someone's mouth is you should not judge. (Mt. 7:1, Lk. 6:37). But how can I be judging when I am only saying what the word of God says. Jesus also said "judge with righteous judgment" (Jn. 7:24).

First of all, what Matthew was saying in Matthew.7:1 and Luke 6:37 is do not judge someone if you are doing the same thing. Some people like to go around trying to find fault with people saying this person is fat so he is ugly or this person eats too much.

Do you eat a lot and sometimes eat the wrong food? Then don't talk about someone else who does that when you may be doing the same thing. Maybe you are overweight or weigh more than you should. If you do, don't talk about someone else if you have the same problem. This is what it means when it says in Luke 6:41 "and why do you look at the speck in your brother's eye, but do not perceive the plank in your own eye."

Now looking at Matthew 7:2, this is why it says: "what judgment you judge, you will be judged and with what measure you use, it will be measured back to you." Because if you are doing the same thing, God is going to judge you as well.

Then, in verse 5 it calls you a "hypocrite! First remove the plank from your own eye, and then you will see clearly to remove the speck from your brother's eye." So, you see from looking at this, God is not saying that you can't judge, so long as you are not doing the same thing. First make sure that you are not involved in this behavior and then you can see clearly to tell your brother not to do it.

Then using John 7:24 as an example, people used to accuse black people of being stupid, or because they came from a certain part of town they must sell or use drugs or steal etc. They were considered bad just because of the color of their skin. That is why Jesus says: "do not judge according to appearance."

Then, it says use righteous judgment. This means don't judge unless you see me stealing or using drugs or fornicating or having sex with the same sex. That is what is meant by judge with righteous judgment.

Jesus was often accused of being led by the devil. (Matt. 9:34, Matt. 12:24). However, Jesus also told them why they were wrong and were not judging righteously (Matt. 12:25-26). He also told them the reason why they were hypocrites. He told them that they were doing the same thing so how can you judge me?

Finally, in verse 28, he tells them how he was doing these things—by the Spirit of God. Furthermore, he was also telling them that they were involved in a grievous sin because they were saying that the power he was using to cast out devils was done by the prince of devils. Because it says in Ephesians 4:30, "Do not grieve the Holy Spirit of God."

This was blasphemy against the Holy Spirit and would not be forgiven in this life or in the life to come. This is the second judgment. This is what is meant by, "it will not be forgiven him, either in this age or in the age to come" (Matt. 12:31-32).

II Kings 18:20 continues, "you speak of having plans for war; but they are mere words. And in whom do you trust, that you rebel against me?"

Just in case you were not aware of it, we are at war with the enemy; that being the devil. It says in Ephesians 6:10-11, "Finally my brethren, be strong in the Lord and in the power of his might. Put on the whole armor of God that you may be able to stand against the wiles of the devil."

First of all, you do not put on armor unless you are ready to go to battle with someone. And that someone has to either die or lose. If you use your armor correctly, which is by faith, that devil has to lose. In II Corinthians 10:3 it says, "For though we walk in the flesh, we do not *war* according to the flesh. Then it goes on to say why in verse four, "For the weapons of our warfare are not carnal but mighty in God for pulling down strongholds."

However, I like how the KJV says it better. "For though we walk in the flesh, we do not war after the flesh; For the weapons of our warfare are not carnal, but mighty through God to the pulling down of strong holds. Instead of making the word strongholds one word, it breaks it up into two. This emphasizes that they are strong and they can have a hold on you.

Also, I used the word die or lose when talking about putting on armor. In the Old Testament, when they put on armor to fight someone died (Jud. 9:54, II Sam. 1:15). However, when you fight against the enemy or devil, which is a spiritual battle, you are not able to kill him; you can only cause him to lose because he will come back again (Lk. 4:13).

Going on with what Sennacherib, who sent his advisors had to say, is that these are mere words (II Ki. 18:20). Hebrews 4:12 says, "For the word of God is living and powerful, and sharper than any two-edged sword." That doesn't sound like mere words to me.

What Sennacherib was saying in effect, is do not fear the words of Hezekiah, who represents the living God, because his words don't mean a thing and can't hurt you. Have you ever heard of the nursery rhyme: "Sticks and stones may break my bones but words will never hurt me"? This is essentially what Sennacherib's person was saying.

Finally, when Sennacherib's person says, "and in whom do you trust, that you rebel against me?" Our trust should be in the Lord our God because everything that He has ever said has come true. This is evident in Isaiah's prophecy concerning the words of God. Isaiah 55:11 says, "So shall my word be that goes forth from my mouth; It shall not return to me void, but it shall accomplish what I please, and it shall prosper in the thing for which I sent it."

In other words, whatever the Lord says will serve a purpose and not be futile or void, but will perform the task in which it was sent to do.

For example, when God created the heavens and the earth, it says in Gen. 1:3, "Then God _said_ let there be light and there was light". Then in verses 6-7 of the same chapter it says, "Then God _said_ Let there be a firmament in the midst of the waters, and let it divide the waters from the waters. Thus, God made the firmament, and divided the waters which were under the firmament from the waters which were above the firmament; and it was so."

Also in John, and this is the only place where this is recorded; Jesus said who do you seek and they said

Jesus of Nazareth, and after Jesus said: "I am He" they all fell to the ground including Judas (Jn. 18:4-6). The reason why they fell down is because Jesus' words were so powerful.

Jesus was also saying what His father said over 4,000 years ago. Moses was keeping his father in law's Jethro's sheep and he came across this bush that was burning with fire but the bush was not consumed. When he went over there to get a closer look, this is when God spoke to him (Ex. 3:1-6) (Ex. 3:1-6).

Moses continues to have a conversation with God and asked what is your name and what should I say has sent me? God says in Exodus 3:13-14, Then Moses said to God "Indeed, when I come to the children of Israel and say to them, "The God of your fathers has sent me to you, and they say to me, "What is His name? What shall I say to them?" And God said to Moses "I AM WHO I AM" And he said "Thus you shall say to the children of Israel, I AM has sent me to you."

If you continue to read on about this story, everything that God said would happen to Egypt happened. Once again, God's words do not come back to Him void.

Finally, continuing with 2 Kings 18:20, where it says, "in whom do you trust, that you rebel against me?" Like I said before, we trust in the Lord our God and we will certainly rebel against you if what you say is against God's law or what He isn't saying.

In the book of Acts, the apostles were being singled out for preaching in the name of Jesus. The authorities of that day were saying that they could not do this. But Peter had something else to say. Starting in Acts 5:12, "And through the hands of the apostles many signs and wonders were done among the people. And they were all with one accord in Solomon's Porch."

Skipping down to verse 17, "Then the high priest rose up and all those who were with him which is the sect of the Sadducees, and they were filled with indignation, and laid their hands on the apostles and put them in the common prison."

Then in verse 19, "But at night an angel of the Lord opened the prison doors and brought them out, and said, "Go, stand in the temple and speak to the people all the words of this life."

Going down to verse 28, "saying, Did we not strictly command you not to teach in this name? And look, you have filled Jerusalem with your doctrine, and intend to bring this Man's blood on us!"

Verse 29 is the verse I really want you to see: "But Peter and the other apostles answered and said, "we ought to obey God rather than man."

Therefore, those are my words even to President Obama. We must obey God's words rather than man.

Showing Love

Now others will also say that you are not acting in love when you say those type of things about the homosexuals. My answer to that is if I didn't love them I wouldn't say anything at all. In John 15:12-13, it says, "This is my commandment, that you love one another as I have loved you. Greater love has no one than this, than to lay down one's life for his friends."

The reason why I say this is because I am certain to get a lot of flak and ridicule as well as attacks over this book. However, according to John 15:14; I do it anyway because God told me to write it and because I love the homosexual too. "You are my friends if you do whatever I command you."

There was a time when even Jesus' own family stood outside seeking to talk to Him. They were attempting to stop Him from talking about the word of God to the people. However, He told them that those who do the will of God are his brother's sister's and mother. (Mk 3:31-35). So, know that unless you do what God has told you to do, you do not belong to Him. You are no longer a part of His family.

Once again it says that you cannot love God Who you have not seen, without first loving your brother whom you have seen (I Jn. 4:20-21). So, if I fail to love the homosexual, even though what they are doing is wrong, I cannot in all sincerity say that I love God whom I have never seen.

The word also says in John's gospel, "For God did not send His Son into the world to condemn the world, but that the world through Him might be saved" (Jn. 3:17). Similarly, I am not trying to condemn the homosexual but trying to help them see the light.

This is evident in the story concerning Saul's conversion who later became Paul (Acts 9:1-6). (Acts 9:1-6). Then it says in verse 8 that when he opened up his eyes he was blind and needed others to lead him by the hand.

Finally, after God reaches out to Ananias, he prays over Saul who later receives his sight and becomes baptized (Acts 9:10-18). (Acts 9:10-18)

In this story, the homosexuals are the ones who are blinded and I, as it were, am the one praying and reaching out to them so that they may receive their sight from being spiritually blinded. Then after receiving their sight, they can once again have right fellowship with God by being baptized.

Chapter 5

People In The Church Who Twist The Words of God

I told you I would discuss further in greater detail what that scripture meant by the devil twisting God's words found in Psalm 91:11-12. There are men in the church (meaning ministers of the Gospel) who want to water down the words of God to help their church grow and to please the people so they can ultimately get more money from them.

Jesus called himself the Good Shepherd (Jn. 10:11). For Jesus to say good must mean that there have been bad ones out there as well. Jesus also said in that same verse that He gives his life for the sheep. This specifically means that when He died on the cross, He was giving his life for all of his sheep or people who would believe in His name.

The word *sheep* here is referring to His (or God's) people. The word shepherd is referring to men of God in the pulpit.

David realized this more than anyone because he was once a shepherd boy (I Sam. 17:34-35). He explained to Saul, Israel's first king, that he gave or risked his life for the sheep.

Then later on in his life, after David became King David, he wrote Psalm 23, one of the most-quoted scriptures in the Bible. King David was well aware that God was his shepherd.

The sheep is a dumb animal and has to be directed to do everything—that is what is meant by "Your rod and your staff they comfort me." If you did not watch over them well, they could get out of sight and be lost. Jesus knew this too, which is why He used that in some of His parables to the people (Matt. 18:12).

Jesus also knew that some shepherds were just hirelings and were not the true shepherd. A hireling is just doing it for the money. John 10:12 says, "But a hireling, he who is not the shepherd, one who does not own the sheep, sees the wolf coming and leaves the sheep and flees; and the wolf catches the sheep and scatters them."

This is essentially saying that first of all, a hireling is not the shepherd because he does not truly care for the people (or sheep). Second, he does not own the sheep as he has only been hired to do a job. That is like people that have a church and want to find a preacher to lead them. They will search for a preacher that is saying the things that they want to hear, otherwise, they will get rid of him.

Third, when the devil (or the wolf) attacks the church regarding money that they may owe or people get filled with evil spirits that can't be controlled, they end up leaving because they don't have the means to combat that attack or run out of money to pay the preacher and he leaves because he was only in it for the money anyway.

Fourth and finally, because the preacher left the church because of evil spirits or because there was not enough money to pay him, the devil scatters the church so they all run to different churches that are once again saying the things that they want to hear.

Therefore, whatever he tells you is to get your money or keep you interested (Job. 7:2) "Like a servant who earnestly desires the shade, and like a hired man who eagerly looks for his wages." What this is essentially saying is that this servant wants it easy by always being in the shade and then wants to get paid quickly. He does not want to be out in the heat of the day where it is hard and sometimes dangerous because all he's really after is the money.

In 2 Timothy 4:3 it says, "For the time will come when they will not endure sound doctrine, but according to their own desires, because they have itching ears, they will heap up for themselves teachers." This is essentially saying that they will not hear the word of truth but believe in a lie. If a man of God or anyone else comes to you and says that it is not wrong to be with another man, that is a lie from the pit of hell. This is similar to, "they will not endure or (listen to) sound doctrine, but according to their own desires."

People who listen to these preachers have a desire to be with the same sex. Therefore, they seek out people who are talking like that. This is what it means when it says in 2 Timothy 4:3) "They will heap for themselves teachers." Heap means to accumulate further or seek additionally. In other words, there will be more and more people who will begin talking this way.

It also says in Galatians 1:8, "But even if we, or an angel from heaven, preach any other gospel to you than what we have preached to you, let him be accursed."

In other words, if another preacher (which signifies we) or an angel from heaven (the devil who I told you earlier was originally in heaven) preach any other gospel (another name for the word of God) than what we have preached to you (nowhere in the Bible can you find it where it says it is okay for a man to marry a man or for a woman to marry another woman), let him be accursed.

Accursed in the Greek means to be excommunicated, cursed or banned. So, that is how we as children of God should treat people (especially preachers representing God) that try to say that God doesn't mind if they (men with men or women with women) marry each other.

When the devil tried to get Jesus to throw himself off of the pinnacle of the temple, and then quoted him the Psalm 91 as evidence of that statement that was the devil twisting the word of God.

I once heard a person over the radio reference Leviticus 18:22, "You shall not lie with a male as with a woman." This person had the audacity to say that he didn't lie with a man like a woman. He lies with a man like he lies with a man. That is twisting the word of God to mean something it never was intended to mean. Anyone who believes that way is also doing exactly what the devil did to Jesus in the wilderness when he said that statement concerning the Psalm 91.

Being Set Apart for God

This is also a good time to talk about people in the church who either sing, usher, lead praise and worship and don't have their lives right with God. Meaning, they are involved in some sort of sexual sin, perversion, homosexuality or other form of fornication.

First of all, looking at the Old Testament, to do the work of God in the Temple, you must be sanctified.

In Hebrew this word is *qadash* which means to make, pronounce or observe as clean both morally and ceremonially. An example of this was when Aaron and his sons were being sanctified or set apart for the work that God was going to have them do (Lev. 8:30, Num. 7:1). In Numbers, ceremonial sanctification where everything that was to be used for the Lord had to be sanctified and consecrated to him. Both of these words (sanctified and consecrate), come from the same root word which is *qadash*.

In the New Testament, the word *sanctified* is taken from the Greek word *haglazo.* This also means to make holy, purify or consecrate. An example of this is in John 17:19 where Jesus is talking and says: "And for their sakes I sanctify Myself, that they also may be sanctified by the truth." This means that Jesus made himself holy or purified himself so that he could sanctify others by the truth which is what he taught them.

Jesus made himself holy by praying to the Father by himself (Mk. 1:35); (Lk. 5:16; Lk. 6:12).]He only spoke what He heard the Father speak (Jn. 12:50, Jn. 8:26).

As far as Christians are concerned we should work to be used for honor (2 Tim. 2:20-21); "But in a great house there are not only vessels of gold and silver, but also of wood and clay, some for honor and some for dishonor. Therefore, if anyone cleanses himself from the latter, he will be a vessel for honor, sanctified and useful for the Master, prepared for every good work."

This means that in the body of Christ, (which is that great house), there are vessels made of gold and silver. This means that they are used for special purposes. Then there are other items that are made out of wood and clay, which are not used for anything special. In other words, they will probably not be in God's house. So, if we work hard to be those items made out of gold and silver, which is the first part the word was referring to, then we will also be used by the Master or (Christ), because we have prepared ourselves for every good work.

It also states, "For both He who sanctifies and those who are being sanctified are all of one, for which reason he is not ashamed to call them brethren" (Heb. 2:11). This means that we are one in Christ if we are sanctified (or clean) and by that happening, Jesus is not afraid to call us His brethren. Or Romans 8:29b, "that he might be the firstborn among many brethren." This means that Jesus was the first to die and everyone who died or lived in Him became part of His family as well.

Therefore, you cannot be sanctified or clean if you are fornicating, or having sex with the same sex or trying to become a woman when in fact you are a man (which is what the transvestites do), or say that God made a mistake when He created you a man but you say you are a woman or vice versa (which is what the transgender do), or are involved in any kind of adultery.

First Corinthians 10:7-11is a marvelous passage of scripture because it merges the Old and New Testaments. It says, "And do not become idolaters as were some of them. As it is written, The people sat down to eat and drink, and rose up to play. Nor let us commit sexual immorality, as some of them did, and in one day twenty-thousand fell; nor let us tempt Christ, as some of them also tempted, and were destroyed by serpents; (according to Num. 21: 7-9) nor complain as some of them also complained and were destroyed by the destroyer." You can read all about this in Exodus 32.

Verse 11 continues, "Now all these things happened to them as examples, and they were written for our admonition, upon whom the ends of the ages have come." This simply means that we are living in the last days and that is why this is being written so that we may know not to do these things.

Skipping down to verse 13, "No temptation has overtaken you except such as is common to man; but with the temptation will also make the way of escape, that you may be able to bear it." This simply means don't think you are the only one that gets tempted. God has given you resources in His word that can combat anything that the enemy puts against you.

For example, God says in 1 John 4:4, "Ye are of God, little children, and have overcome them; because greater is He that is in you than he that is in the world. When the word says, *them* he means anyone that is of the enemy. You can overcome them because Jesus overcame them. Didn't Jesus also say: "Verily, verily, I say unto you, He that believeth on me, the works that I do shall he do also; and greater works then these shall he do because I go unto my father." (Jn. 14:12). Jesus defeated the enemy in Matthew 4. If He did it, you can do it too.

Finally, regarding this subject, let me leave you with this last scripture found in Ephesians 5:3, which says, "But fornication and all uncleanness or covetousness, let it not even be named among you, as is fitting for saints." This is pretty self-explanatory but all of the bad things mentioned above should not be happening among people who call themselves Christians or saints.

Just in case you were not aware, the word *Christian* comes from a Greek word *Christianos*, which literally means Christ like or a follower of Christ. So, whatever Christ did is what you should be doing as well.

The word *saints* comes from another Greek word in the New Testament called *haglos* meaning sacred, blameless or most holy thing. So, that is what we are and what we are called to be according to 1 Corinthians 1:2 that says, "To the church of God which is at Corinth, to those who are sanctified in Christ Jesus, called to be saints, with all who in every place call on the name of Jesus Christ our Lord, both theirs and ours."

Even though he was talking to the people of Corinth, he also said to those who are sanctified in Christ Jesus. If you have been saved or gone through the conversion process, similar to what Paul went through, then you have now been sanctified by Jesus Christ.

After being sanctified, you are also called to be saints, which once again is blameless or a most holy thing. Once again he says: "with all who call on the name of Jesus Christ our Lord."

Just in case you don't think that he is talking about you he uses the word *all*—that means everyone who calls on the name of Jesus. Then, he puts a comma there to signify that he is not through. He ends the statement by saying "both theirs and ours." This means to both the people in Corinth, which is who the letter was written for, as well as to us meaning those people who are not necessarily in Corinth, but still call on that name which is Jesus Christ, whomever they may be.

Chapter 6

The Bible and Civil Rights

The Lord is all about civil rights concerning Him and His people. When I say His people, I mean all that want and have a desire to serve Him in spirit and in truth as stated in John 4:24) where it says: "God is a Spirit, and those that worship Him must worship Him in spirit and truth." However, I like how the KJV says it better when it says, "God is a Spirit: and they that worship Him must worship Him in spirit and in truth." *In truth* is what I want you to see.

Anyone can worship God or a (god), but are they doing it according to the truth? The nation of Israel, for example, saw that Moses (the man of God) had gone up into Mount Sinai to talk with God (Ex. 24:1-2). Because he had been gone for forty days and nights (Ex. 24:18), the nation of Israel began to get worried.

Then it says in Exodus 32:1, "Now when the people saw that Moses delayed coming down from the mountain, the people gathered together to Aaron, and said to him, Come, make us gods that shall go before us; for as for this Moses, the man who brought us up out of the land of Egypt, we do not know what has become of him."

Then as the story goes, they created a golden calf to represent their god out of all of the jewelry they had. (Ex. 32:2-4). This may have been their god, but it was not the God Who brought them out of the land of Egypt—that part was a lie. A lie is the exact opposite of being the truth.

While we are on that subject of Egypt, why did they have to come out of there? It was all because they were large in number and because they were Jewish. (Ex. 1:7-10). If that wasn't enough, the Pharaoh put taskmasters over them to afflict them with their burdens, and they built for Pharaoh supply cities, Pithom and Raamses (Ex. 1:11).

This sounds very much like what blacks or Negroes had to go through when the United States was being built. They had task masters over them too who watched them as they were out in the fields of Georgia, Mississippi, Alabama etc., picking cotton and building up the Americas.

They also didn't get paid for what they did, which is what happened to the nation of Israel. If that wasn't enough, Pharaoh ordered that all male children be killed before they had a chance to grow (Ex. 1:15-16).

The king of Egypt tried to destroy a race of people known as the Hebrews. This behavior was unjust because it wasn't being done because they were doing something wrong such as having sex with another man or a woman having sex with another woman; but mistreating another person simply because of who he or she was—being Jewish or Hebrew, or as I said before Negro or black.

God also did not say do not lie with a white person as you would a black person or vice versa. God was not interested in skin color when trying to find a mate. This is seen when Moses (the man of God), came into the camp with a black woman from Ethiopia; and Aaron and Miriam, his brother and sister, spoke against Moses because of it. (Num. 12:1-2). In the early years of America, it was against the law for a black man to marry a white woman or vice versa. It did not make any difference how much money you made either; this law applied to them as well.

Then, it says that the Lord heard it and called all three of them out to the tabernacle of meeting to have a discussion with them (Num. 12:4). He had some very important things to say to Aaron and Miriam specifically (Num. 12:6-8). As punishment for talking against the man of God and for getting upset about this Ethiopian woman, God turned Miriam, who probably was the first person to speak against his brother being with this woman, into a leper (Num. 12:9-10).

What God has to say about being married to another person is found in 2 Corinthians 6:14 where it says, "Do not be unequally yoked together with unbelievers." Paul goes on to say, "For what fellowship has righteousness with lawlessness? And what communion has light with darkness?"

A believer is one who believes in Jesus the way you do (Jn. 14:6). This means that you both believe in the death (Jn. 19:30); burial (Jn. 19:42); and resurrection of Jesus (Jn. 20:9); that He died for our sins; (Jn. 3:16); and will soon come back to a church that is without spot or wrinkle (Eph. 5:27). If you both believe that way, then there is no reason why the two of you can't get married. Skin color has nothing to do with it.

When the Bible says what communion does light have with darkness, that simply means that light and dark cannot exist at the same time. Jesus put it this way in John 8:12, "I am the light of the world. He who follows Me shall not walk in darkness, but have the light of life." It does not mean that black and white people cannot be or do things together.

When the Bible uses darkness here, it is not necessarily talking about dark in being lack of sunlight, rather something that is bad or evil for you. Light here means doing godly things or things that can prolong your life. Jesus also said in John

5:24, "Most assuredly, I say to you, he who hears my word and believes in Him who sent me has everlasting life, and shall not come into judgment, but has passed from death into life." As long as you are doing what God wants you to do, you should have a long successful life on this earth. He who walks or follows Christ is the same one who walks in the light of life.

During the early 1960s and 1970s, there was a man by the name of Dr. Martin Luther King Jr., who fought furiously for civil rights but did it non-violently. At that time, segregation existed where blacks and whites had to be separated in everything they did. This involved where they went to the bathroom, where they lived, where they ate and of course where they went to school. Things were so bad that you couldn't even worship God in the same church or drink out of their water fountains. King fought hard against segregation and subsequently was put in jail, talked about by the authorities of that day, and ultimately killed for his beliefs.

Was this man attacked for doing something against the word of God for wanting to live in peace with his fellow man? Was he going against the word of God for wanting to eat or drink where he wanted to? Was it against the word of God for wanting the same education as the white people of his generation?

The answer just in case you weren't aware of it is **no**! God is interested in faith and doing what He has commanded you to do (Heb. 11:6) "For without faith it is impossible to please him." Psalm 119:11 says, "Your word have I hidden in my heart, that I might not sin against you."

During the civil rights movement, it was against the law for a black person to sit in the front of the bus. They would have to pay their fare in the front of the bus and then get off once again and go to the back of the bus. If they were in the black section of the bus and a white person got on and there was no more room for them in the white section, they would make the black person get up and give their seat to him or her.

There was a person by the name of Rosa Parks who was extremely tired from working all day and was sitting in the black section. A white person came on and wanted to sit where she was sitting. She said no and from that day on all hell broke loose. They actually called for the police who told her she had to get up. This is what later on led to the Montgomery Bus Boycott where all blacks decided to boycott the buses and instead walked to wherever they were going.

Were they creating that law because the Lord told them to do it? Is it anywhere in the word of God that says a white person is superior to a black person? I don't think so. My Bible says in Rom. 12:3, "For I say, through the grace given to me, to everyone who is among you, not to think of himself more highly than he ought to think."

It isn't wrong to think highly of yourself, just don't think more highly than you ought to think. In other words, don't think that you are better than someone just because your skin is a different color, or because you live in a certain neighborhood, or even drive a certain car—that doesn't mean anything to God.

Jesus said it this way, "But seek first the kingdom of God and His righteousness, and all these things shall be added to you" (Matt. 6:33).

Chapter 7

Why You Have To Be Born Again

This part of the book is written for those who think that because they believe they have been born a certain way or with certain feelings, that they are not responsible for the way they are.

Let me ask you a question. If everyone that you know has ten fingers and ten toes and you have twelve fingers and twelve toes, would you not find something wrong with that? If God made everyone you know with one head but you have two, would you find something wrong with that?

The word of God says that he made them male and female (Gen. 1:27). However, you were born a man but for some reason as far as you can remember, you feel like you should have been born a woman. Therefore, you begin to wear more makeup, earrings and finally even lipstick. The last thing you finally decide to do is put on a dress and wear a wig. This is essentially how a transvestite thinks.

The transgender is a little bit different. He or she thinks that if they were born one sex, that God somehow made a mistake and they should have been born the opposite sex. If they have enough money, they will even get a sex change, which is an extremely large amount of money. When have you

69

ever known the God of this universe to have ever made a mistake? When has the sun failed to come up in the day or set at night? When has God ever said that something would happen and it never did? When has your heart ever stopped beating?

The reason I ask those questions is because if you did have more than the number of fingers or toes you should have, you should consult a doctor. to get that corrected. Similarly, if you have a problem with the way God made you, you should consult God.

There is nothing wrong with you physically, you just feel that you are in the wrong body or are wearing the wrong clothes or some combination of the two. Was Christ ever confused with who He was? Were any of the early apostles confused with who they were? No! Let's find out why.

Jesus said in John 3:3, "Most assuredly, I say to you, unless one is born again, he cannot see the kingdom of God." The reason why Jesus said that is because the things of God are spiritually discerned. Once you become born again you take on a different spirit. Your mind changes too and you find yourself slowly not wanting the things that used to appeal to you before.

Furthermore, Nicodemus, who was the man Jesus was speaking to when He said this, also wanted to know how a man could be born again when he was old (Jn. 3:4). He wondered if he could he enter a second time into his mother's womb and be born again (Jn. 3:5). "Jesus answered, most assuredly, I say to you, unless one is born of water and the Spirit, he cannot enter the kingdom of God. That which is born of the flesh is flesh and that which is born of the Spirit is spirit. Do not marvel that I said to you, you must be born again."

Jesus was talking about two different things here. When He said "unless one is born of water and the Spirit, he cannot enter the kingdom of God." The water represents water baptism.

When one is water baptized, that is a form of dying to this life or one's self. When a person is baptized, he goes into the water symbolizing death to sin, and when he comes back out again he is alive in Christ. Therefore, he has now entered the kingdom of God spiritually.

In Romans 6:1-4 it says, "What shall we say then? Shall we continue in sin that grace may abound? Certainly not! How shall we who died to sin live any longer in it? Or do you not know that as many of us as were baptized into Christ Jesus were baptized into His death? Therefore, we were buried with Him, through baptism into death, that just as Christ was raised from the dead by the glory of the Father, even so we also should walk in newness of life."

Shall we continue to sin? No, because when we were baptized we essentially died to our former life. When we come out of the water, we are alive once again in Christ. Jesus died on that cross but He came to life again on the third day. Also, water baptism is a form of burial for the Christian. As Christ was buried in that tomb, similarly we were buried as well when we entered that water.

What I am saying to the transvestite and transgender person as well as the homosexual is, come to Christ and be born again. When you tell God that He made a mistake with you when you see Him, will not work.

First of all, we did not make ourselves—God did. It says in Isaiah 64:8; "But now, O Lord, You are our Father, we are the clay, and You our potter." It also says in Romans 9:20, "But indeed, O man, who are you to reply against God? Will the thing formed say to him who formed it, why have you made me like this?"

So, I ask the transvestite and the transgender the same questions: Why are you questioning God concerning the sex that he made you? Do you not realize that God first of all made you, knows why He made you like that (meaning male or female), and also what He wants you to do while you are in that body?

In John. 3:5, the Spirit symbolizes the Holy Spirit that was given in the upper room for the first time in Acts 2:1-4; that is why Jesus told them do not leave Jerusalem until they had been endued with power from on high (Luke. 24:49).

In order to fully enter into the promises of God and even understand his word, you must be filled with the Holy Spirit. Without the Holy Spirit, you would be like the Pharisees and scribes who knew the words of God but could not understand them or correctly interpret them.

Nicodemus was a perfect example of this. Here he is a teacher of Israel and you don't know these things Jesus said to him (Jn. 3:10). Or when the scribes and Pharisees asked him why he didn't ceremonially wash his hands (Mt. 15: 1,2), He answered them according to (Matt. 15:3-9).

Or when the scribes and Pharisees asked to show them a sign; (Matt. 12:38). He answered them according to (Matt. 12:39-40), "But he answered and said to them, an evil and adulterous generation seeks after a sign, and no sign will be given to it except the sign of the prophet Jonah. For as Jonah was three days and three nights in the belly of the great fish, so will the Son of Man be three days and three nights in the heart of the earth."

What Jesus was saying here is you are evil and are showing an attitude of being spiritual adulterers by asking for a sign from heaven after all I have already done for you. This sign they were looking for would have been so amazing that it would have been something to worship. They would have tried to make that sign their god that is why Jesus said you are evil and adulterous for seeking such a thing. That is because spiritual adultery is going after other gods (Ex. 34:15, Judg. 2:17).

For example, he healed every illness known to man, (Matt. 8:16, Matt. 12:15); He raised Lazarus from the dead; (Jn. 11:43-44). He made limbs grow out; (Luk. 6:6, 10); and even gave sight to the blind; (Mk. 8:22-25). Finally, he fed the 5000; (Matt. 14:19-21) and the 4,000; (Matt. 15:34-38).

I hope this book has been a deep source of inspiration to you and that you know the Bible has a lot to say about homosexuality. It does not matter how many people are involved in this practice, it is still wrong. It also does not matter who is saying these things are right. What does matter is what does God say? Even if a church or angel says this is right, it is still wrong. God is a God of love and He loves the homosexual, transvestite and transgender too. God fully endorses civil rights as long as they don't conflict with His laws; and even if you were born this way, you simply must be **born again**!

The Sinner's Prayer

Romans 10:9 says "that if you confess with your mouth the Lord Jesus and believe in your heart that God has raised Him from the dead, you will be saved." I am going to write this prayer that you are to recite and believe:

"Lord Jesus I realize that I am a sinner who needs to come to you wholly and completely. I believe in the death, burial and resurrection of Jesus Christ and that He is coming back for me one day. I also ask that you receive me into Your kingdom. In Jesus name. Amen."

Printed in Great Britain
by Amazon

68614405R00047